ELVIS PRESLEY
Favorites FOR GUITAR

ARRANGED BY MARCEL ROBINSON

2   ALL SHOOK UP

6   ARE YOU LONESOME TONIGHT?

12   CAN'T HELP FALLING IN LOVE

9   CRYING IN THE CHAPEL

14   DON'T

17   DON'T BE CRUEL
(TO A HEART THAT'S TRUE)

20   HEARTBREAK HOTEL

22   I WANT YOU, I NEED YOU, I LOVE YOU

25   IF I CAN DREAM

30   IN THE GHETTO
(THE VICIOUS CIRCLE)

34   IT'S NOW OR NEVER

37   KENTUCKY RAIN

42   LOVE ME TENDER

44   LOVING YOU

46   MEMORIES

50   MY

All Shook Up

Words and Music by Otis Blackwell and Elvis Presley

Drop D Tuning:
① = E ④ = D
② = B ⑤ = A
③ = G ⑥ = D

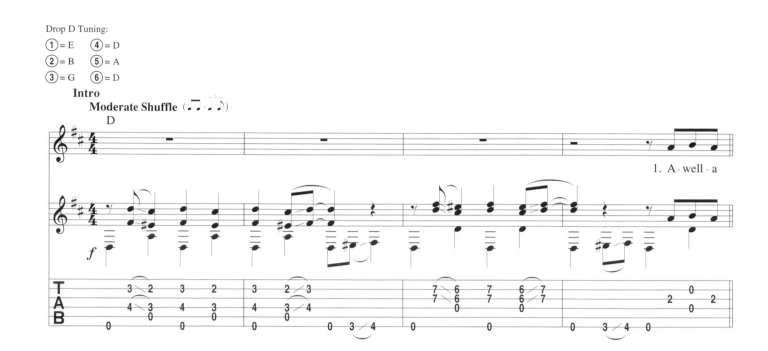

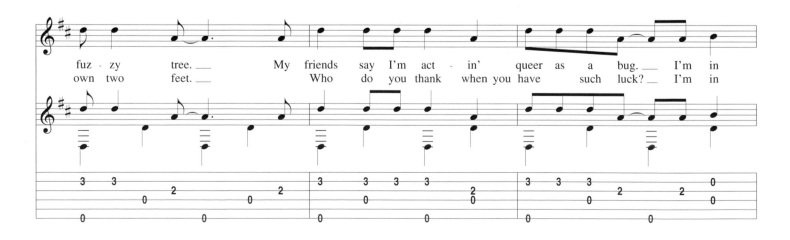

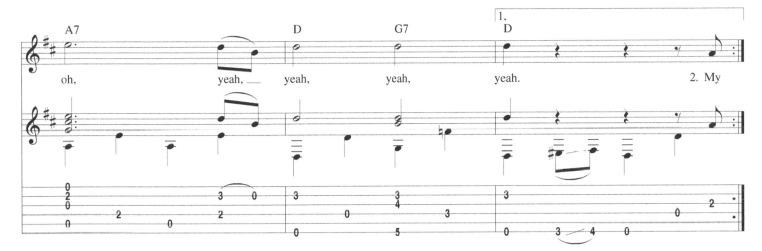

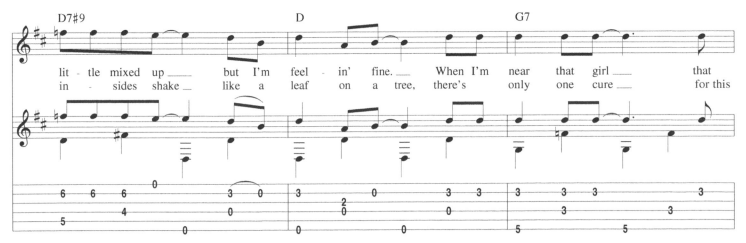

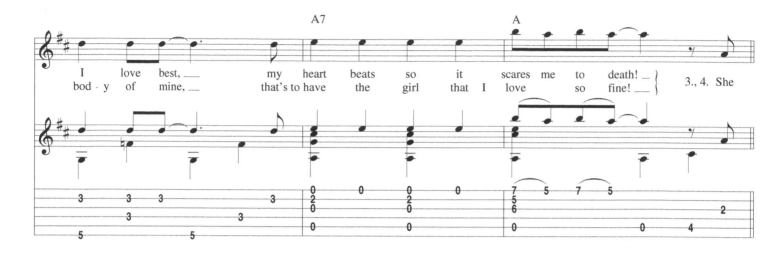

I love best, ___ my heart beats so it scares me to death! ___
bod - y of mine, ___ that's to have the girl that I love so fine! ___
3., 4. She

Verse

touched my hand, what a chill I got. ___ Her lips are like ___ a vol -

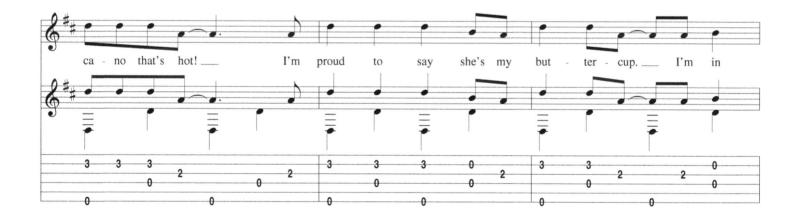

ca - no that's hot! ___ I'm proud to say she's my but - ter - cup. ___ I'm in

love, I'm all shook up! Mm ___ mm, ___ oh

Are You Lonesome Tonight?

Words and Music by Roy Turk and Lou Handman

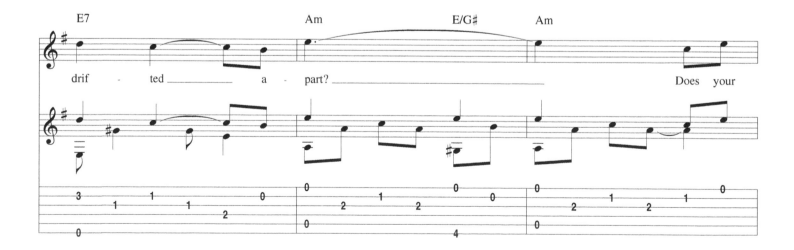

mem - o - ry stray to a bright sum - mer

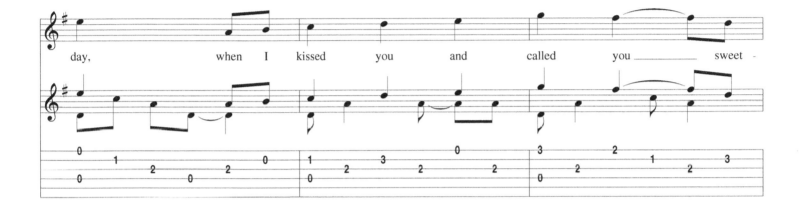

day, when I kissed you and called you _____ sweet -

heart? _____ Do the chairs in your

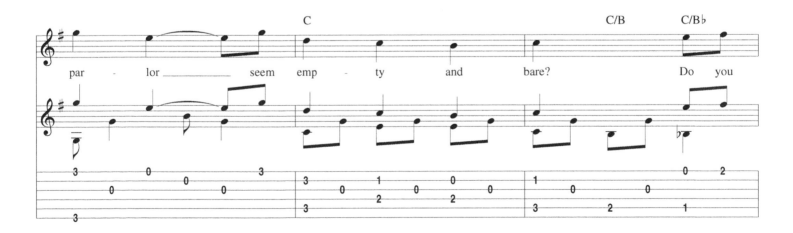

par - lor _____ seem emp - ty and bare? Do you

gaze at your door - step _____ and pic - ture me

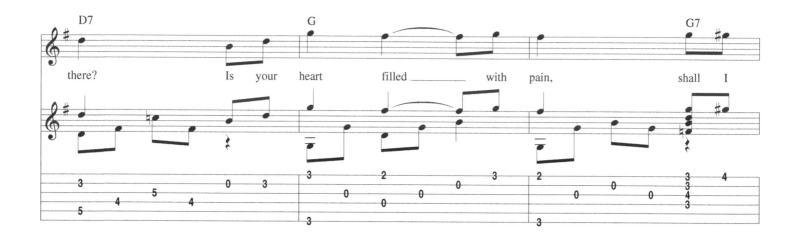

there? Is your heart filled _____ with pain, shall I

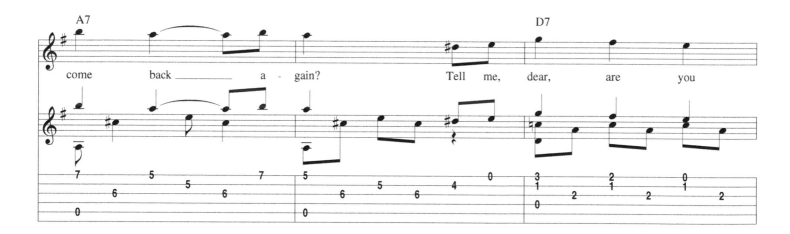

come back _____ a - gain? Tell me, dear, are you

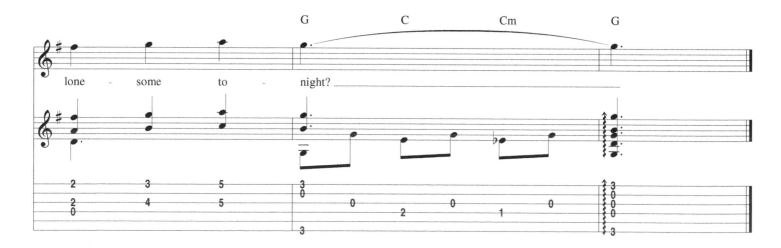

lone - some to - night? _____

Crying in the Chapel

Words and Music by Artie Glenn

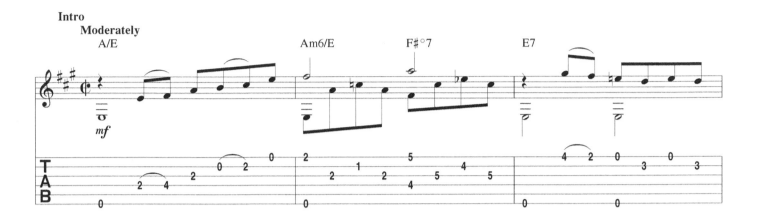

1. You saw me cry-ing in the chap - el, _____ the tears I shed were tears of
some - thing _____ that will put his heart at

joy. _____ I know the mean-ing of con-tent - ment,
ease. _____ There is on-ly one true an - swer,

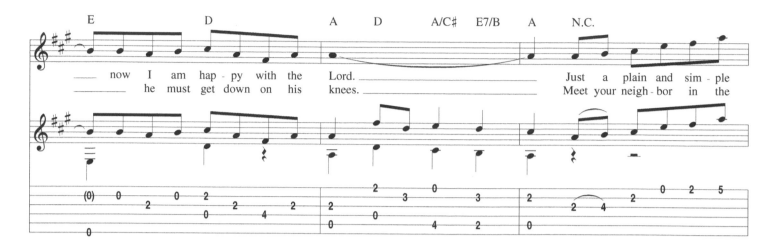

now I am hap-py with the Lord. _____ Just a plain and sim-ple
he must get down on his knees. _____ Meet your neigh-bor in the

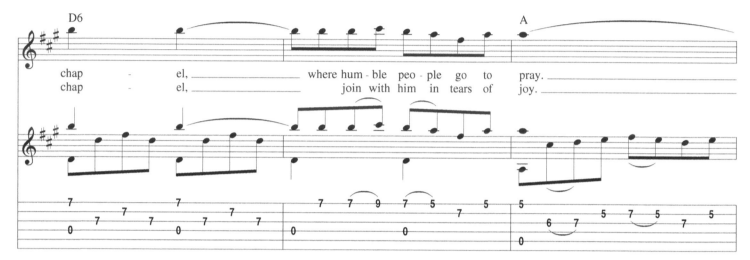

chap - el, _____ where hum-ble peo-ple go to pray. _____
chap - el, _____ join with him in tears of joy. _____

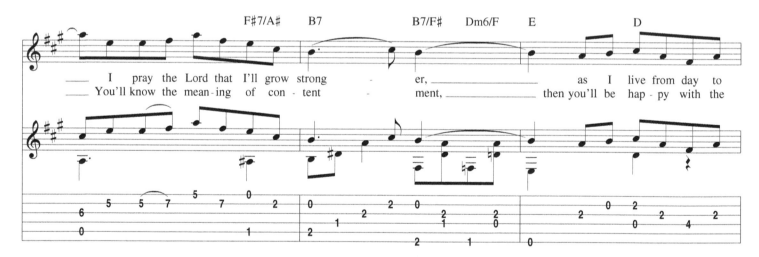

_____ I pray the Lord that I'll grow strong - er, _____ as I live from day to
_____ You'll know the mean-ing of con-tent - ment, _____ then you'll be hap-py with the

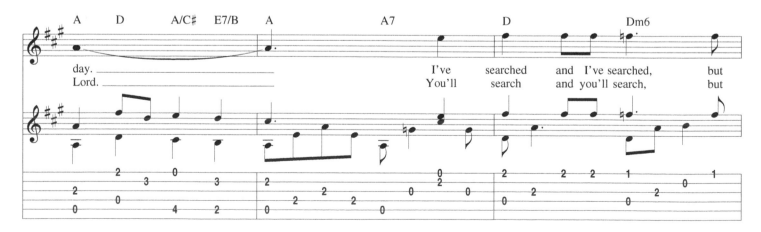

day. _____ I've searched and I've searched, but
Lord. _____ You'll search and you'll search, but

Can't Help Falling in Love

from BLUE HAWAII

Words and Music by George David Weiss, Hugo Peretti and Luigi Creatore

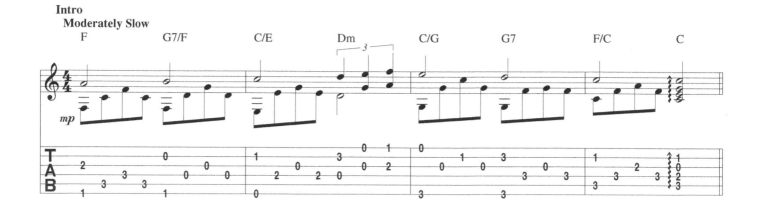

Bridge

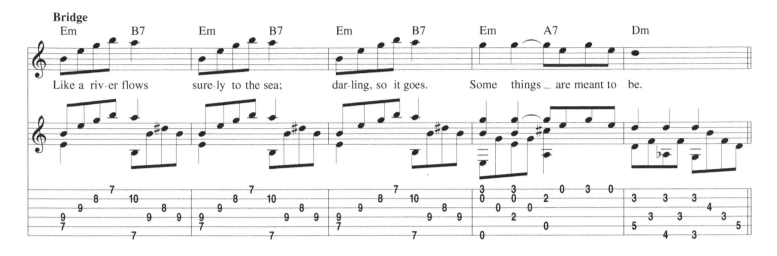

Like a riv-er flows sure-ly to the sea; dar-ling, so it goes. Some things __ are meant to be.

Verse

3. Take my hand, take my whole life too. For

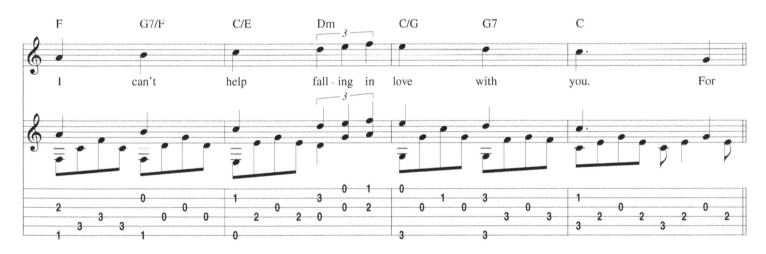

I can't help fall-ing in love with you. For

Outro

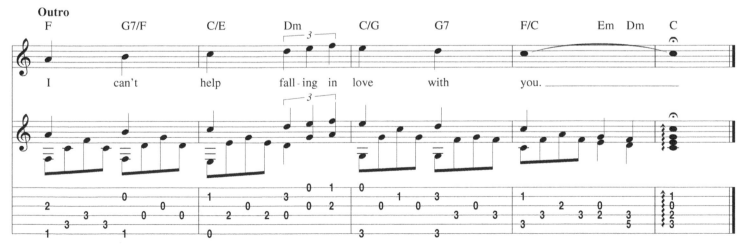

I can't help fall-ing in love with you. _____

Don't

Words and Music by Jerry Leiber and Mike Stoller

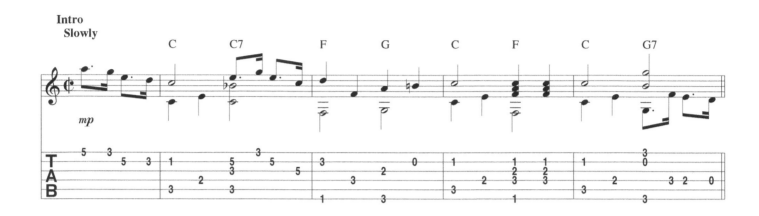

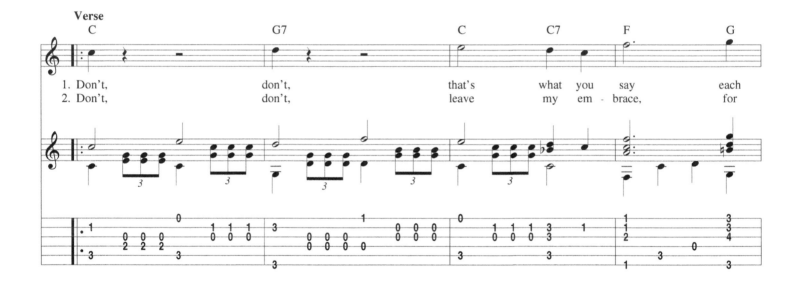

1. Don't, don't, that's what you say each
2. Don't, don't, leave my em - brace, for

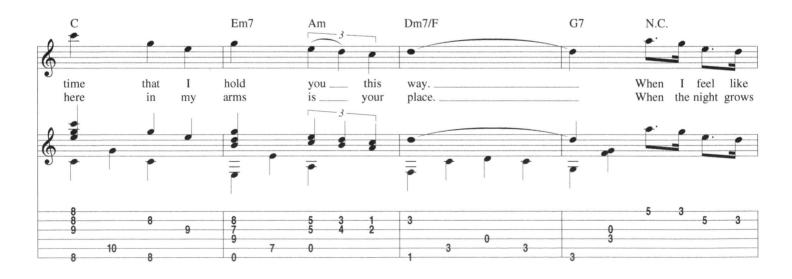

time that I hold you this way. When I feel like
here in my arms is your place. When the night grows

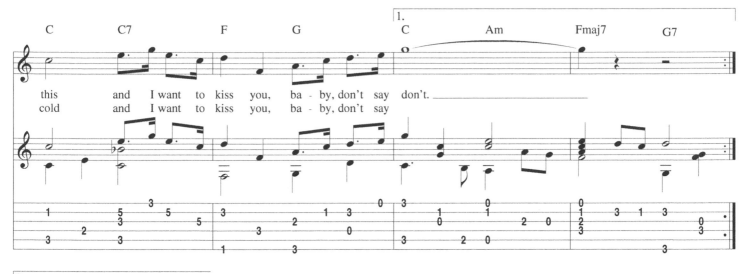

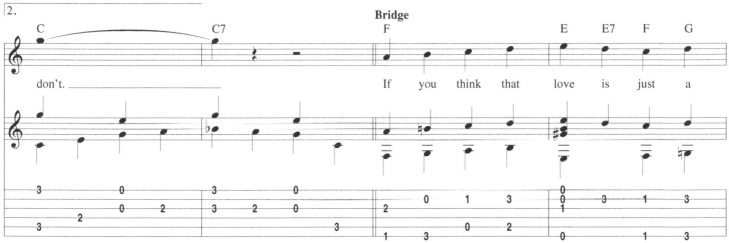

Outro

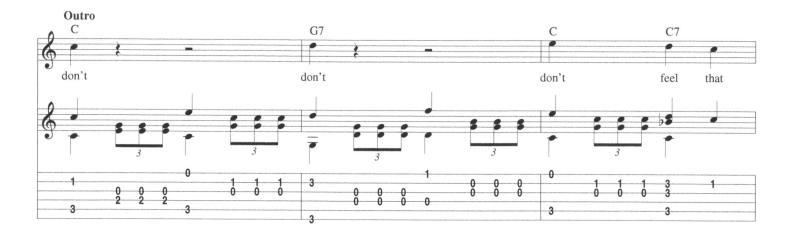

don't   don't   don't   feel   that

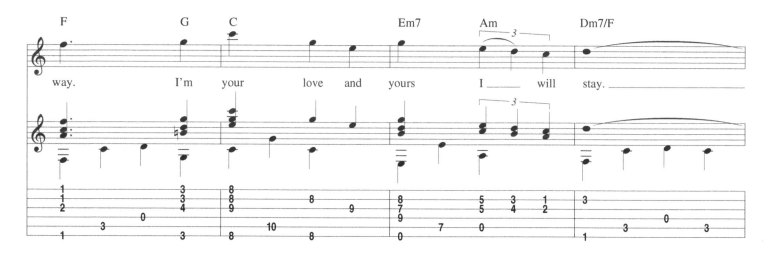

way.   I'm   your   love   and   yours   I ____ will   stay. ____

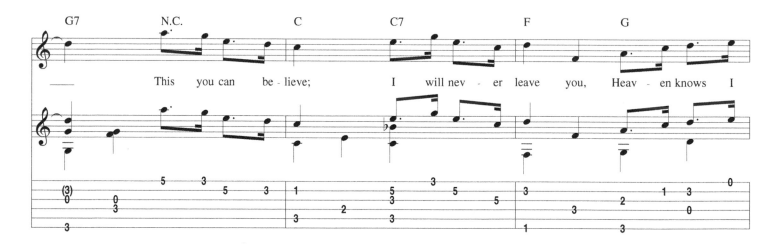

This   you can be - lieve;   I   will nev - er leave   you,   Heav - en knows I

won't. ____   Ba - by, don't   say   don't. ____

16

Don't Be Cruel
(To a Heart That's True)

Words and Music by Otis Blackwell and Elvis Presley

cruel _____ to a heart that's true.
cruel _____ to a heart that's

true. _____ Don't want no oth - er love,

D.S.
(take 2nd ending)
2nd time, D.S. al Coda
(take 2nd ending)

To Coda ⊕

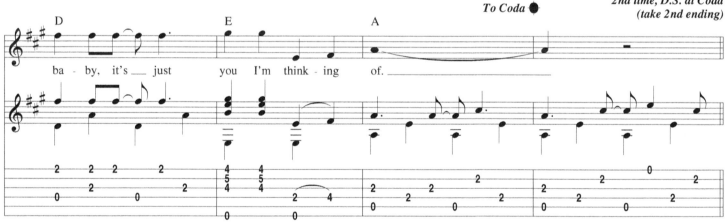

ba - by, it's ___ just you I'm think - ing of. _____

⊕ *Coda*

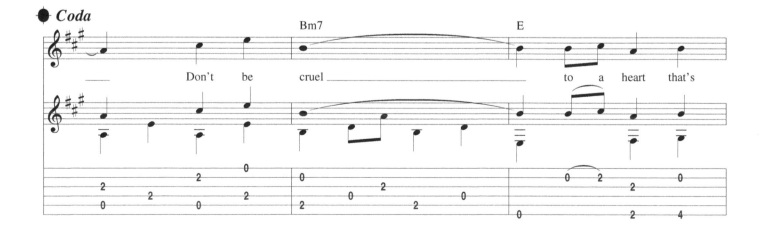

___ Don't be cruel _____ to a heart that's

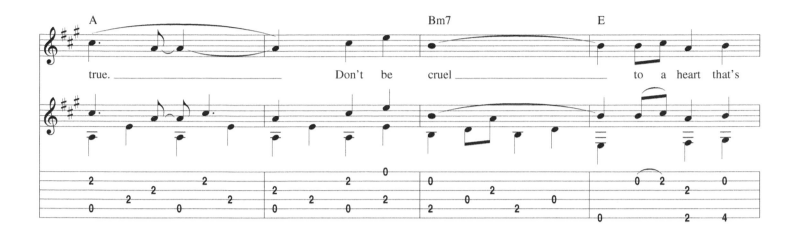

true. _____ Don't be cruel _____ to a heart that's

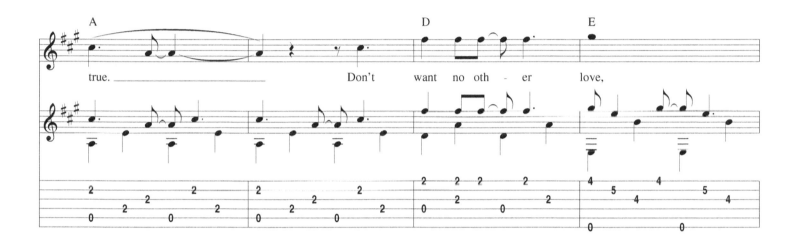

true. _____ Don't want no oth - er love,

ba - by, it's ___ just you I'm think - ing of. _____

Additional Lyrics

3. Don't stop thinking of me,
   Don't make me feel this way.
   Come on over here and love me,
   You know what I want to say.
   Don't be cruel to a heart that's true.
   Why should we be apart?
   I really love you baby, cross my heart.

4. Let's walk up to the preacher,
   And let us say, "I do."
   Then you'll know you have me,
   And I'll know I have you too.
   Don't be cruel to a heart that's true.
   Don't want no other love,
   Baby, it's just you I'm thinking of.

Heartbreak Hotel

featured in the Motion Picture HONEYMOON IN VEGAS

Words and Music by Mae Boren Axton, Tommy Durden and Elvis Presley

Drop D Tuning:
① = E ④ = D
② = B ⑤ = A
③ = G ⑥ = D

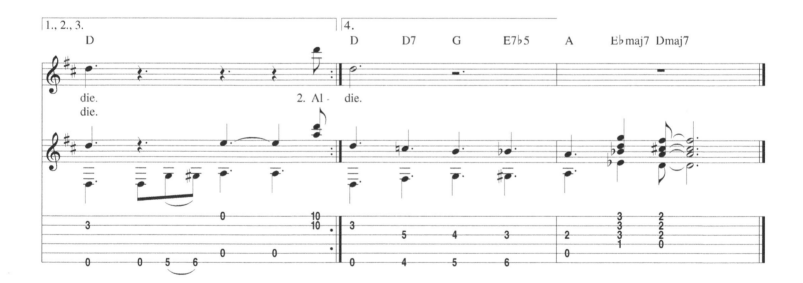

Additional Lyrics

3. Now, the bellhop's tears keep flowing, the desk clerk's dressed in black.
   They've been so long on Lonely Street they'll never, never look back, and they're so,
   And they're so lonely, oh, they're so lonely,
   They're so lonely, they could die.

4. Well now, if your baby leaves you and you've got a tale to tell,
   Well, just take a walk down Lonely Street to Heartbreak Hotel, where you will be,
   You'll be so lonely, baby, well, you'll be lonely,
   You'll be so lonely, you could die.

I Want You, I Need You, I Love You

Words by Maurice Mysels
Music by Ira Kosloff

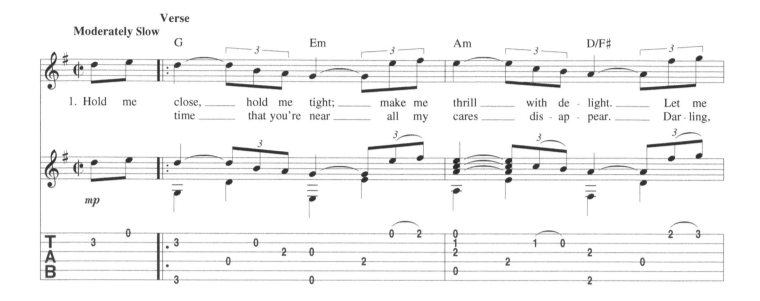

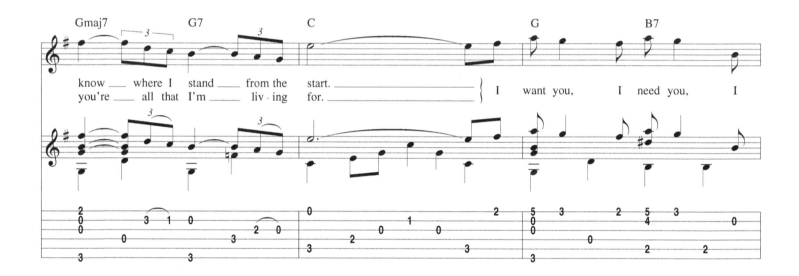

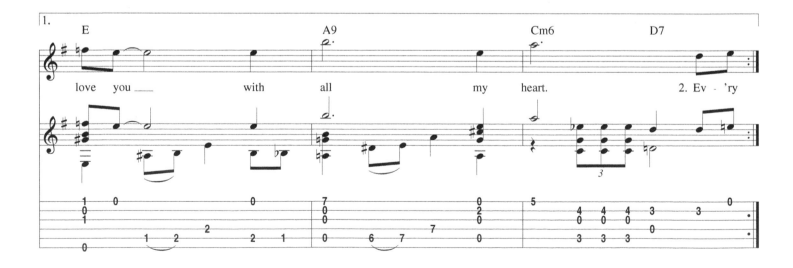

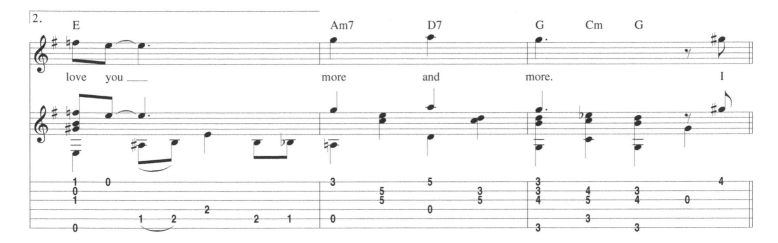

love you ____ more and more. I

Bridge

thought ____ I could live ____ with - out ro - mance ____ be -

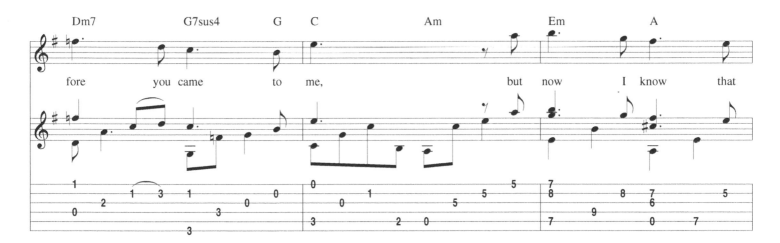

fore you came to me, but now I know that

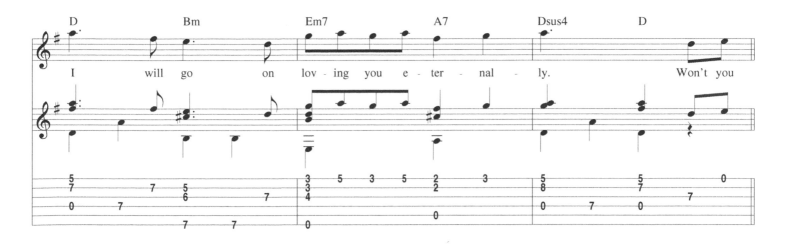

I will go on lov - ing you e - ter - nal - ly. Won't you

Outro

please _____ be my own? _____ Nev - er leave _____ me a - lone, _____ 'cause I

die _____ ev - 'ry time _____ we're a - part. _____ I want you, I need you, I

love you _____ with all my heart.

If I Can Dream

Words and Music by W. Earl Brown

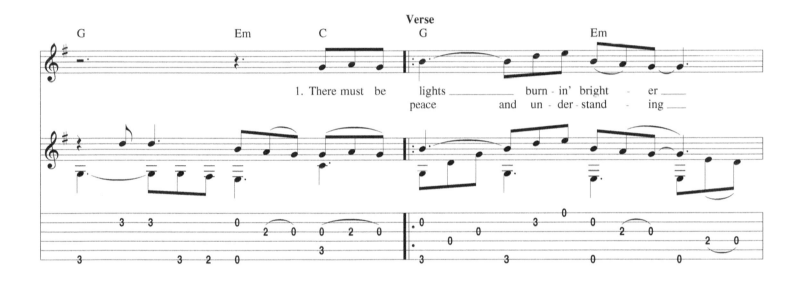

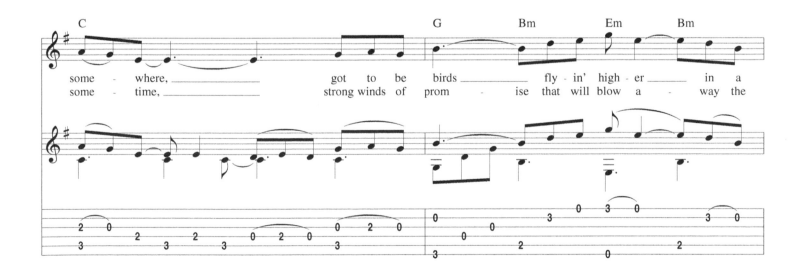

sky _____ more blue. If I can dream _____ of a bet-ter land, __ where
doubt _____ and fear. If I can dream _____ of a war-mer sun, __ where

all my broth-ers work hand in hand, } tell me why, _____ oh, __ why, _____ oh, __
hope keeps shin-in' on ev - 'ry-one, }

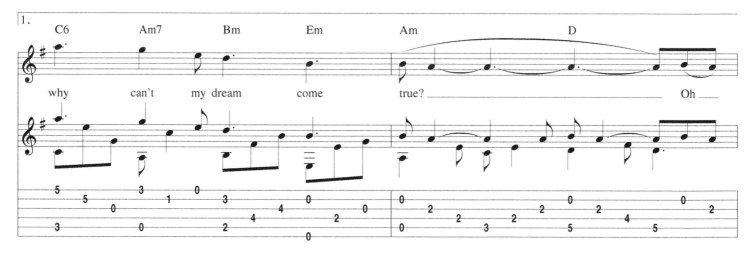

1.

why can't my dream come true? _____ Oh __

why? _____ 2. There must be why _____ won't that sun ap

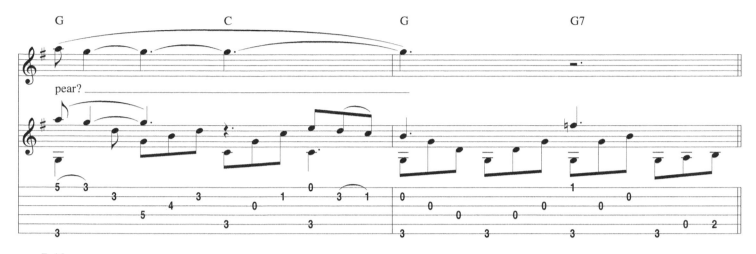

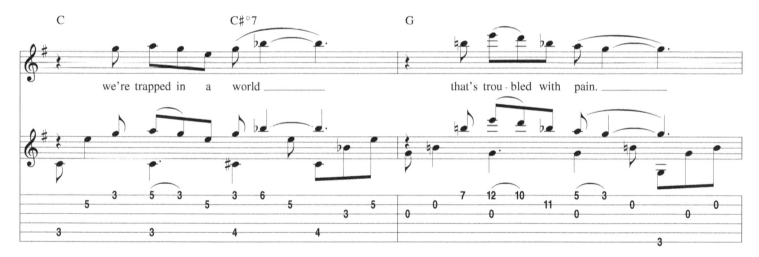

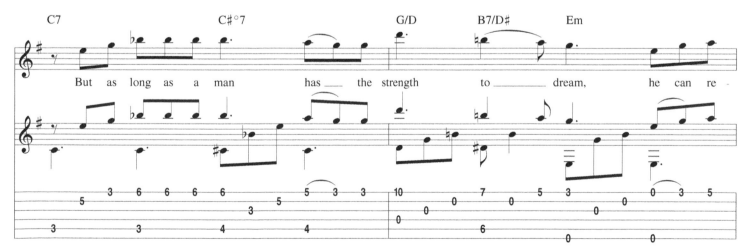

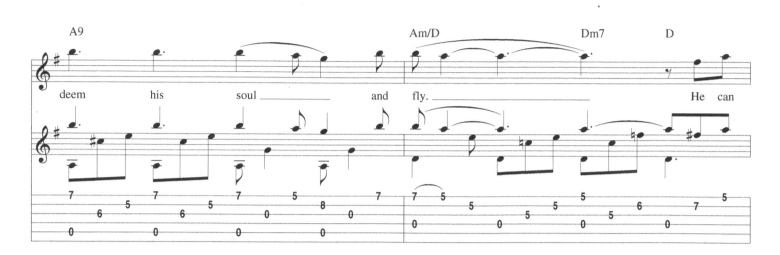

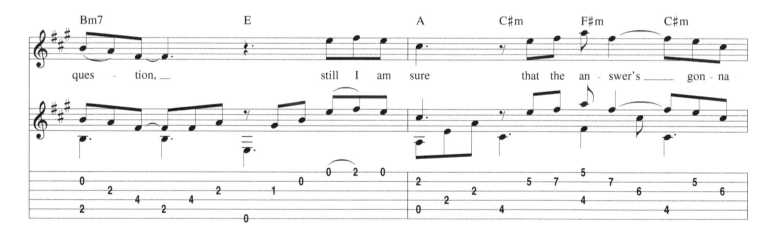

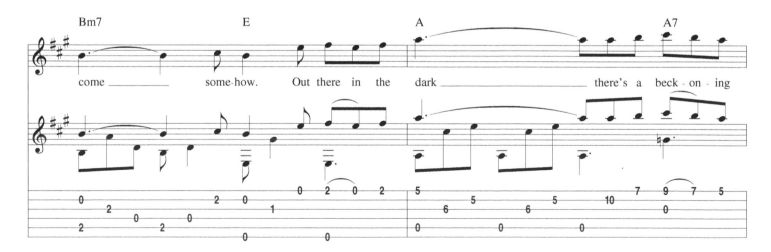

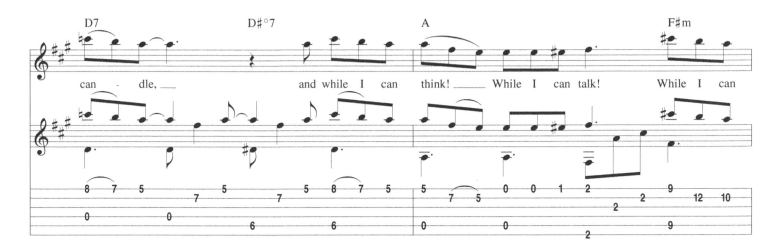

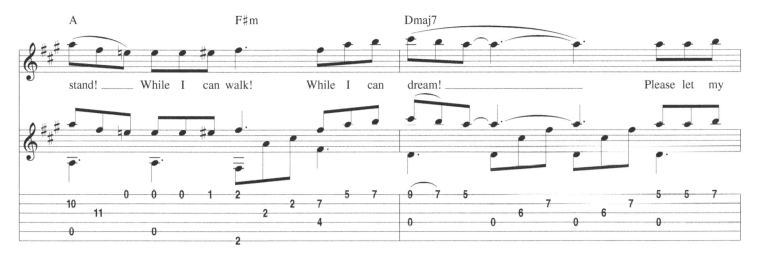

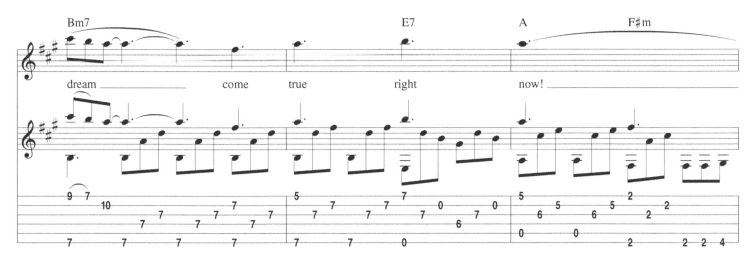

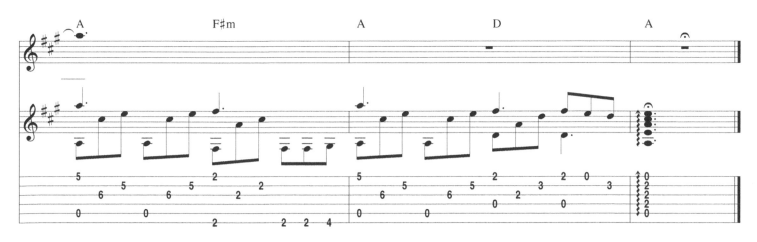

In the Ghetto
(The Vicious Circle)

Words and Music by Mac Davis

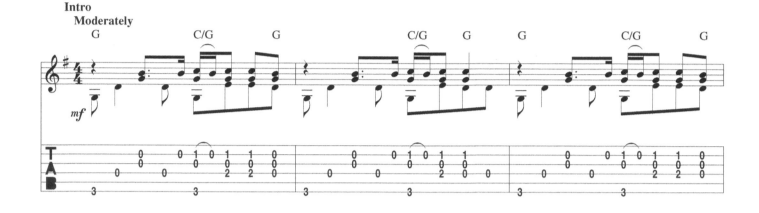

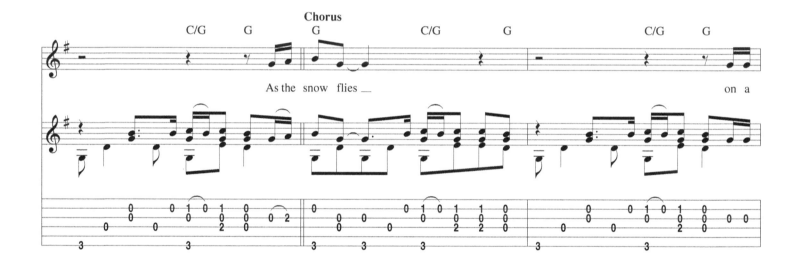

As the snow flies ___ on a

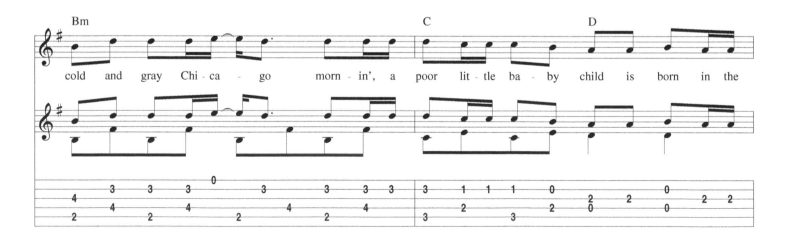

cold and gray Chi-ca-go morn-in', a poor lit-tle ba-by child is born in the

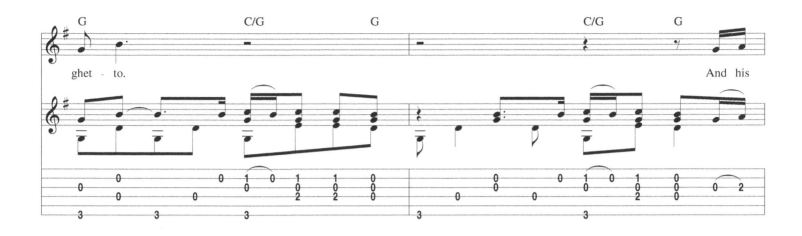

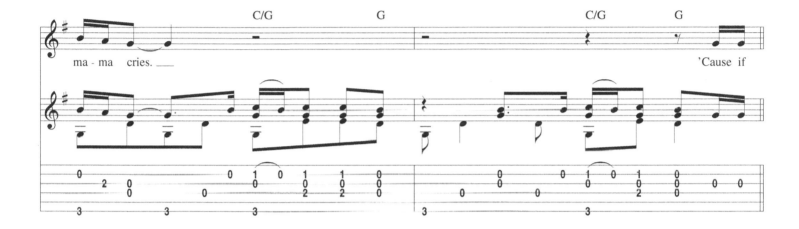

Bridge

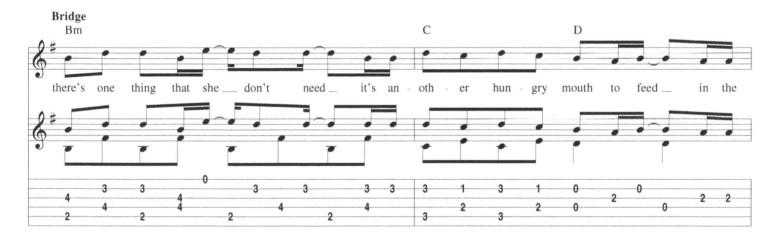

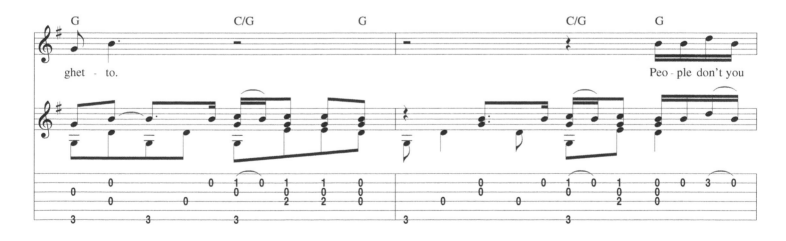

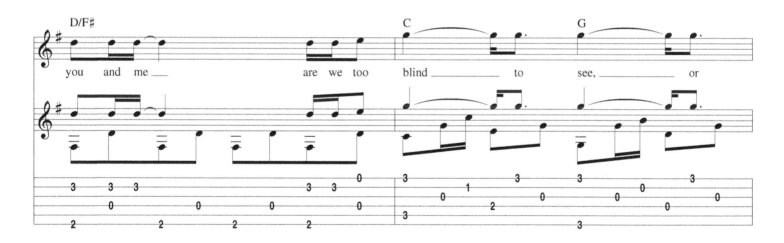

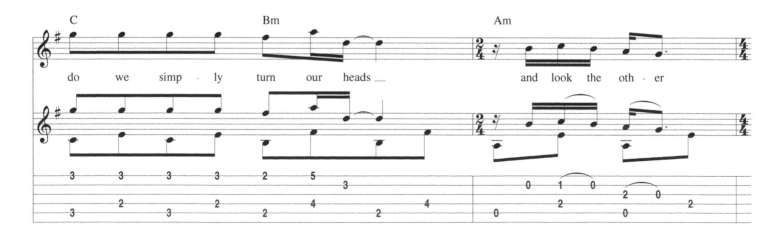

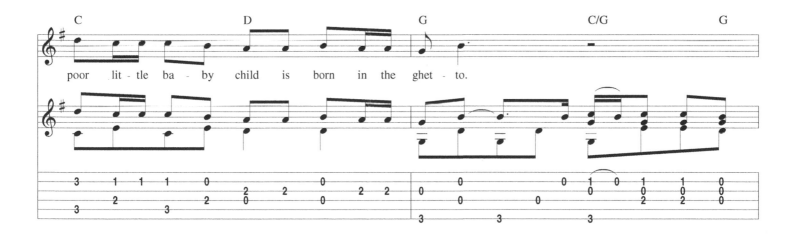

It's Now or Never

Words and Music by Aaron Schroeder and Wally Gold

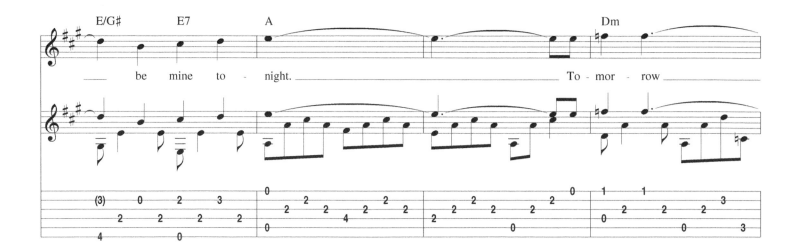

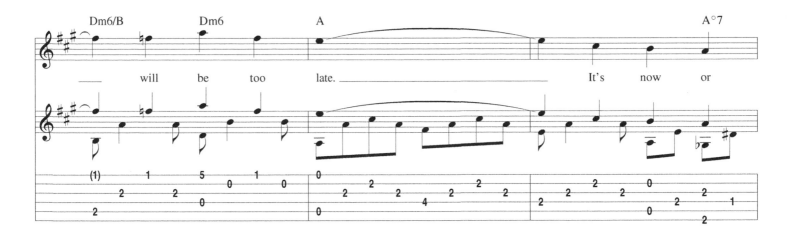

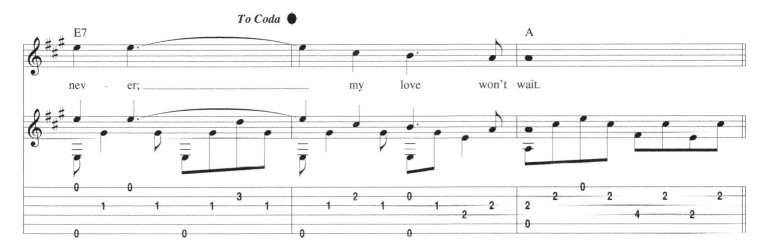

2nd time, D.C. al Coda

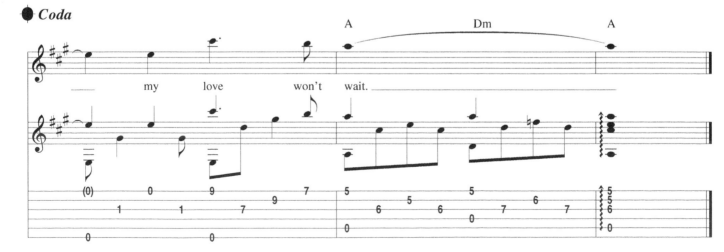

Kentucky Rain

Words and Music by Eddie Rabitt and Dick Heard

1. Sev - en lone - ly days _____ a doz - en towns a - go. _____ I
2. Showed your pho - to - graph _____ to some old gray beard - ed men _____ sit - ting

reached out _____ one night and you were gone.
on a bench out - side a gen - 'ral store.

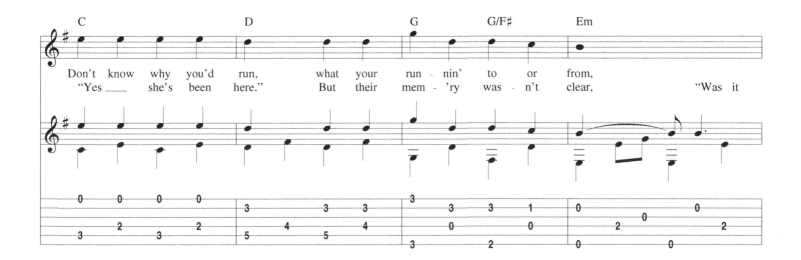

Don't know why you'd run, what your run - nin' to or from,
"Yes _____ she's been here." But their mem - 'ry was - n't clear, "Was it

all I know is I want _____ to bring you
yes - ter - day? No _____ wait, _____ the day be

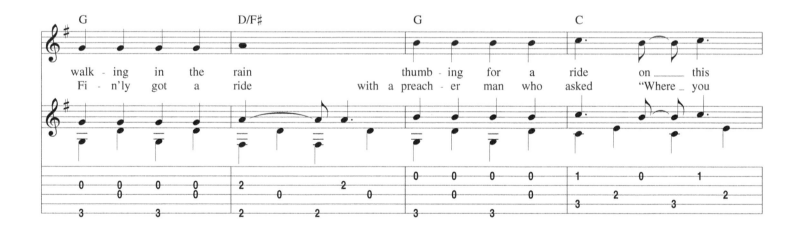

home. So I'm
fore."

walk - ing in the rain thumb - ing for a ride on _____ this
Fi - n'ly got a ride with a preach - er man who asked "Where _ you

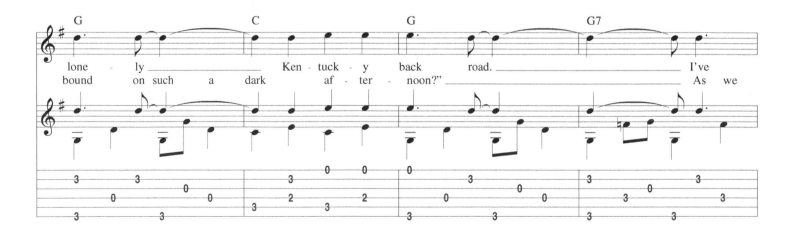

lone - ly _____ Ken - tuck - y back road. _____ I've
bound on such a dark af - ter - noon?" _____ As we

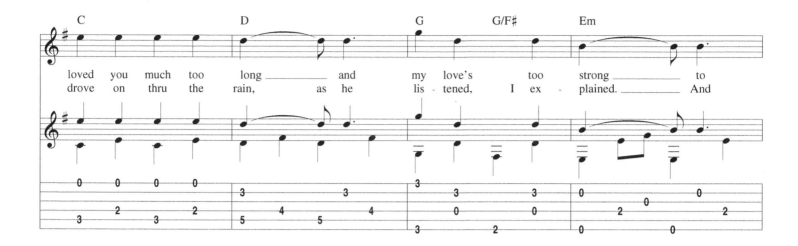

loved you much too long _____ and my love's too strong _____ to
drove on thru the rain, as he lis - tened, I ex - plained. _____ And

let you go. Nev - er know - ing what went
he left me with a pray - er that I'd find

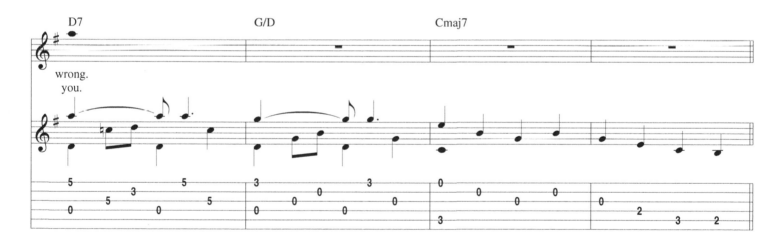

wrong.
you.

Chorus

Ken - tuck - y rain keeps pour - ing down. _____

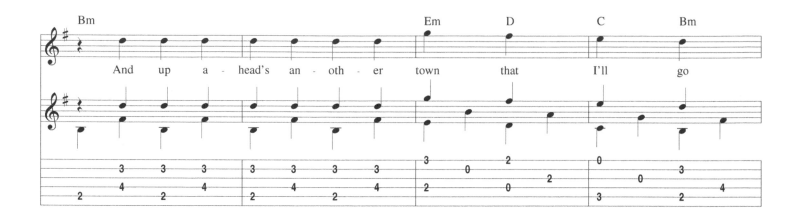

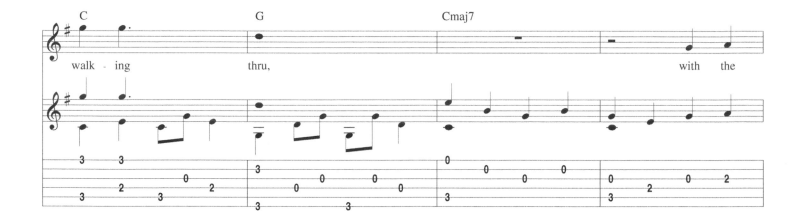

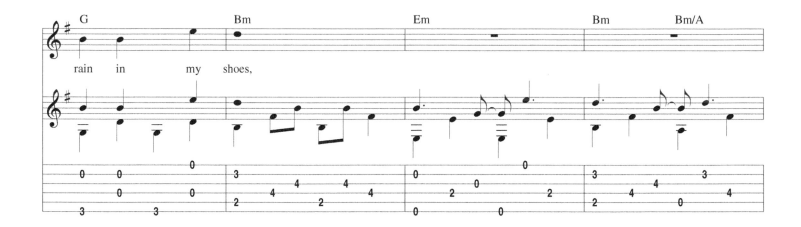

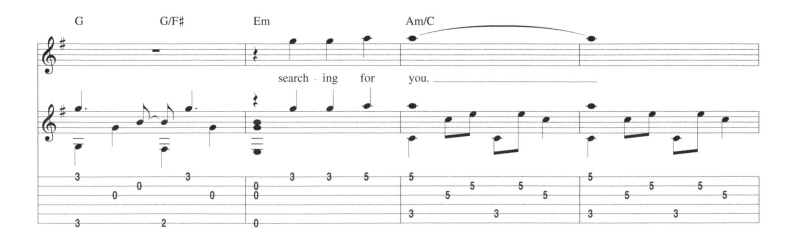

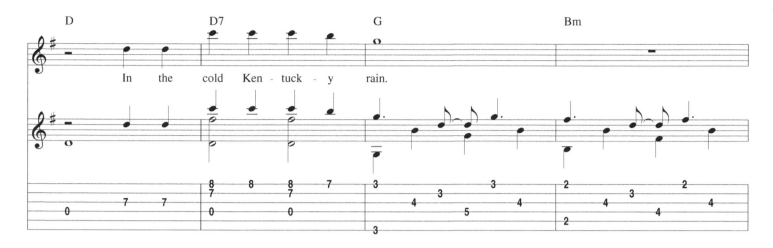

In the cold Ken - tuck - y rain.

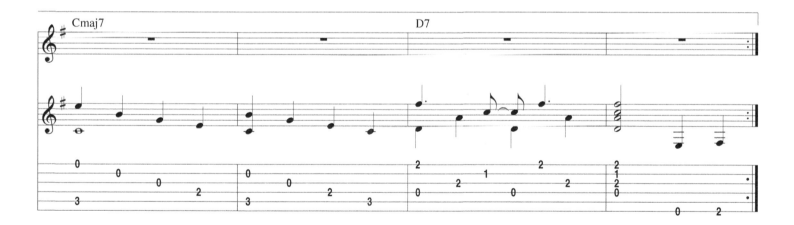

In the cold Ken - tuck - y rain.

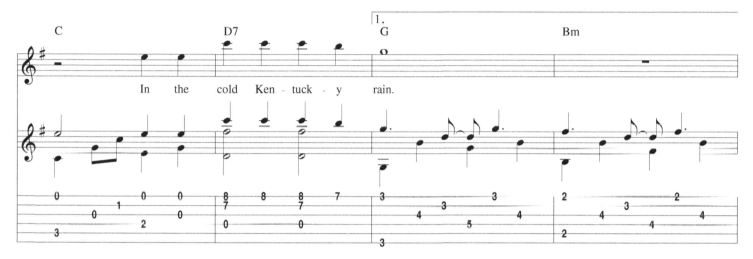

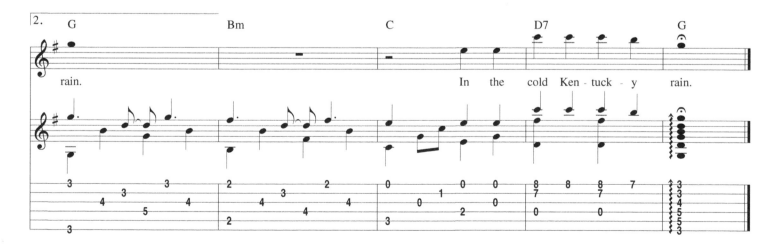

rain.

In the cold Ken - tuck - y rain.

Love Me Tender

Words and Music by Elvis Presley and Vera Matson

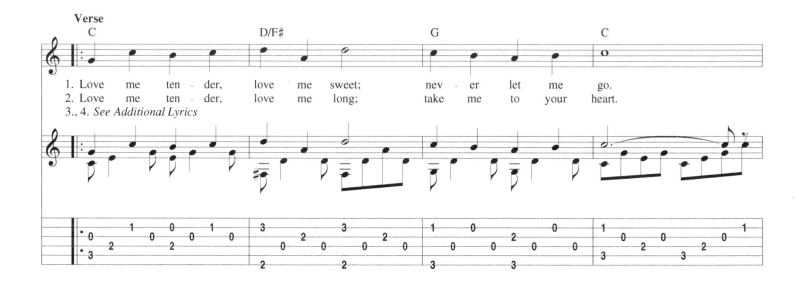

1. Love me ten - der, love me sweet; nev - er let me go.
2. Love me ten - der, love me long; take me to your heart.
3., 4. *See Additional Lyrics*

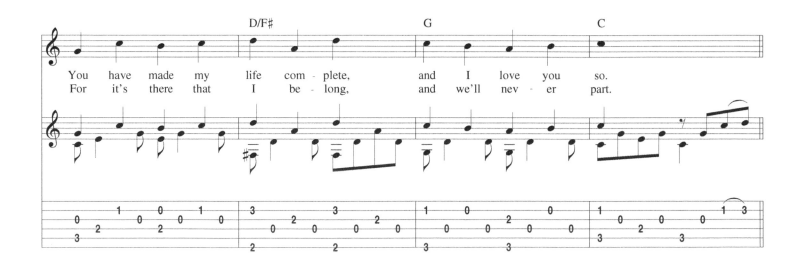

You have made my life com - plete, and I love you so.
For it's there that I be - long, and we'll nev - er part.

Love me ten - der, love me true, all my dreams ful - fill.

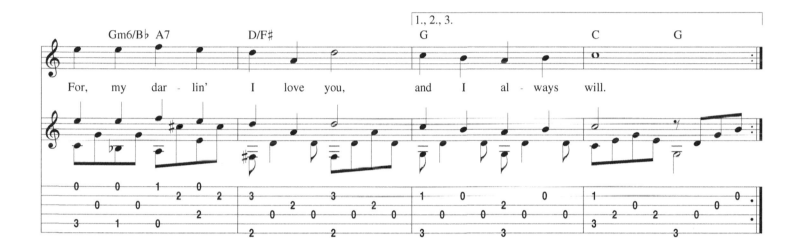

For, my dar - lin' I love you, and I al - ways will.

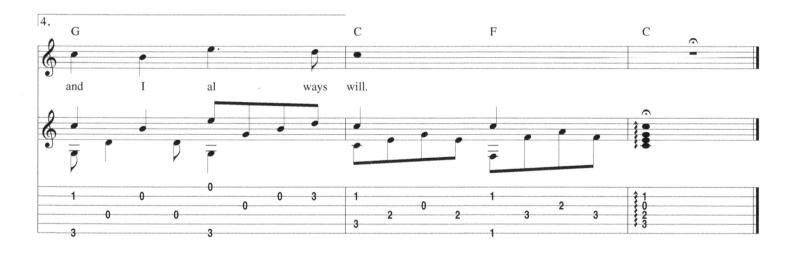

and I al - ways will.

Additional Lyrics

3. Love me tender, love me dear,
   Tell me you are mine.
   I'll be yours through all the years,
   Till the end of time.

4. When at last my dreams come true,
   Darling this I know:
   Happiness will follow you,
   Ev'rywhere you go.

Loving You

Words and Music by Jerry Leiber and Mike Stoller

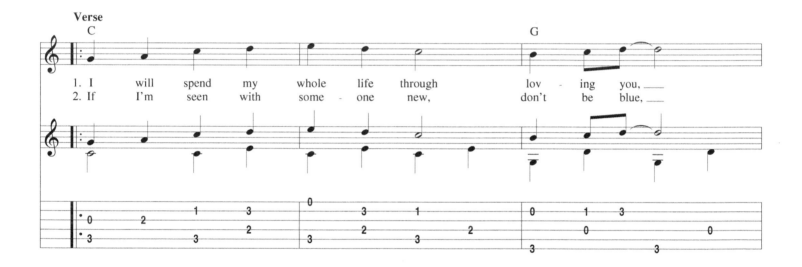

1. I will spend my whole life through lov - ing you, ___
2. If I'm seen with some - one new, don't be blue, ___

lov - ing you. ___ Win - ter, sum - mer, spring - time too,
don't be blue. ___ I'll be faith - ful, I'll be true;

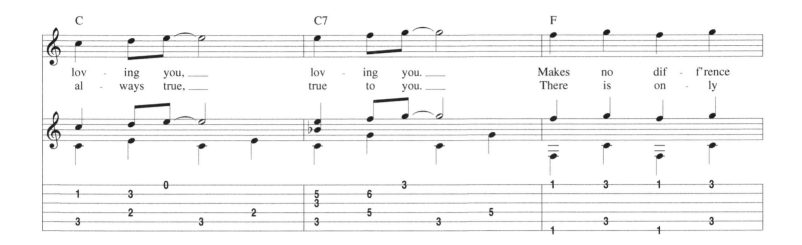

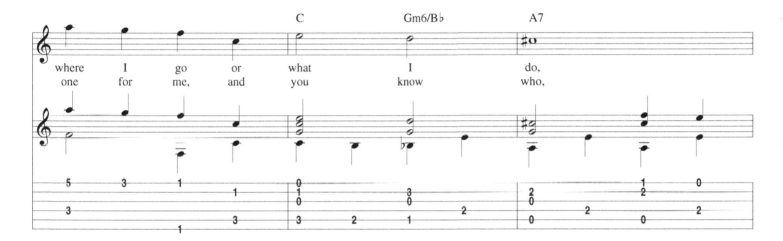

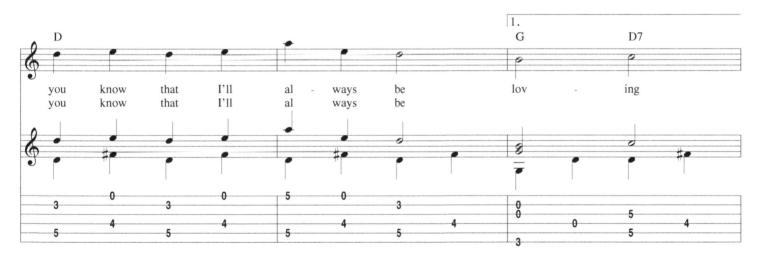

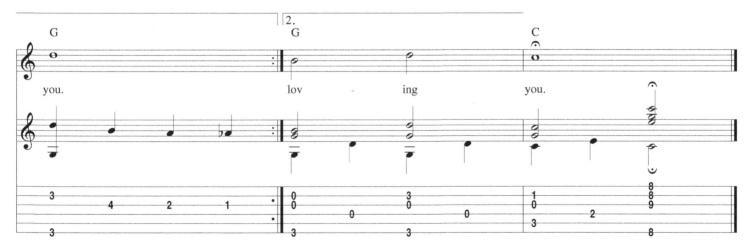

Memories

Words and Music by Billy Strange and Scott Davis

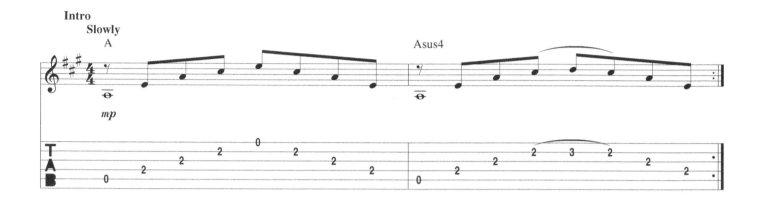

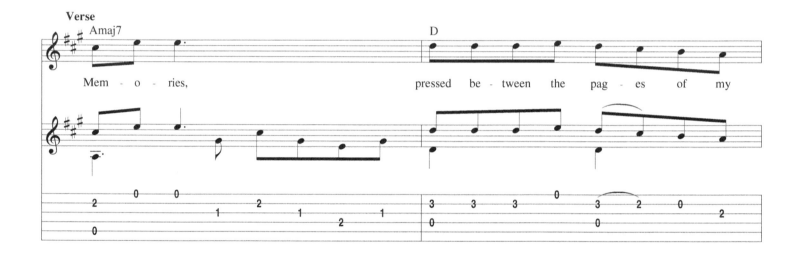

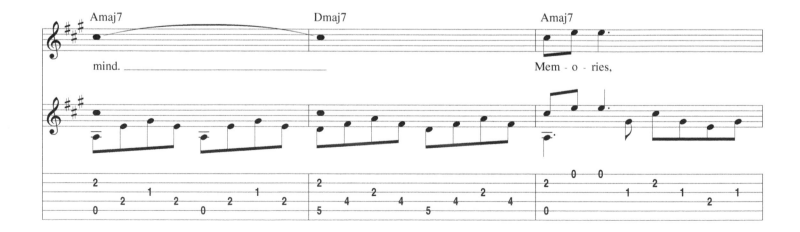

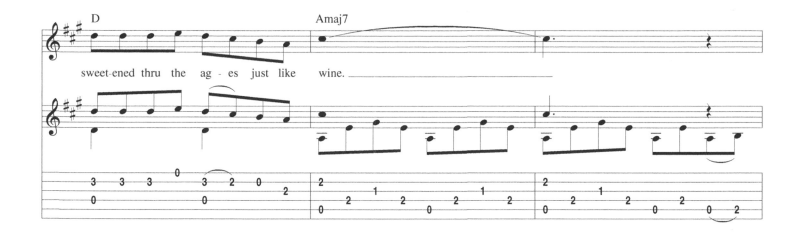

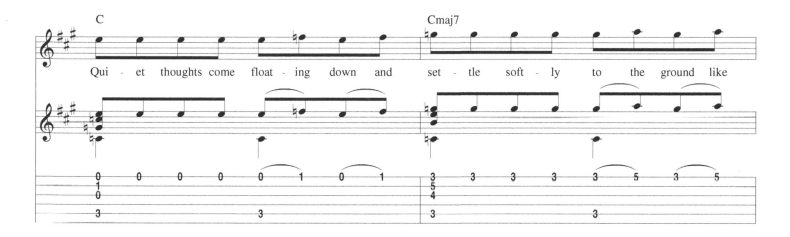

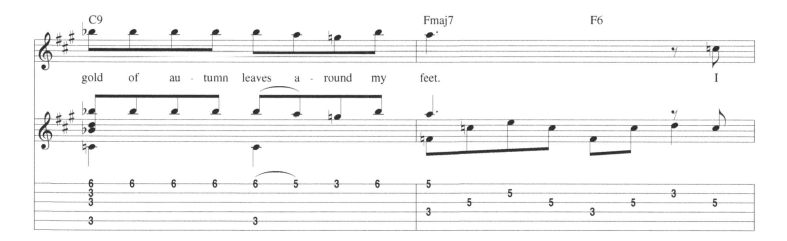

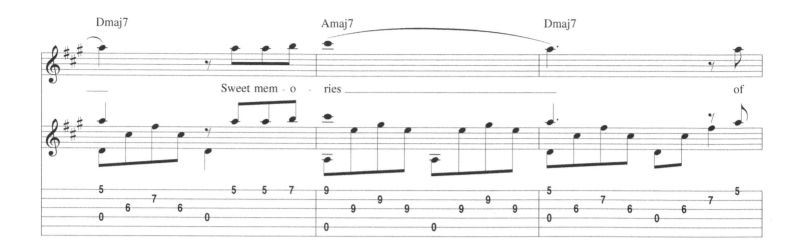

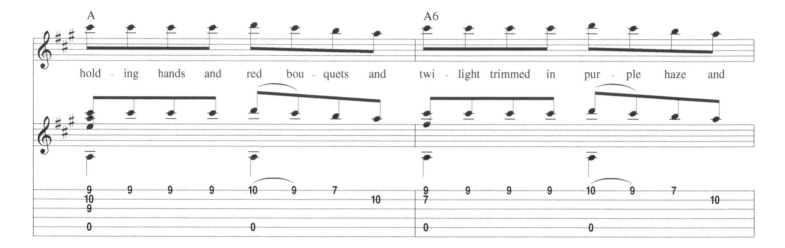

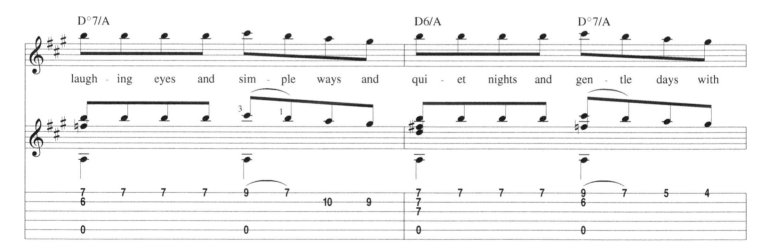

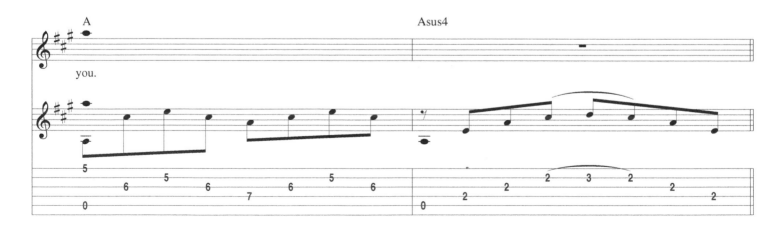

Outro

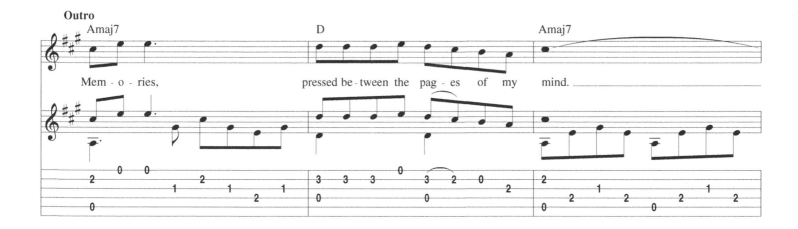

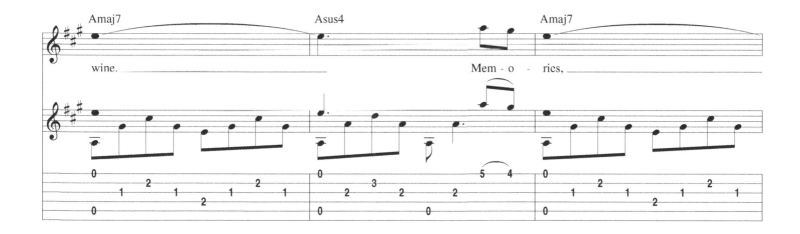

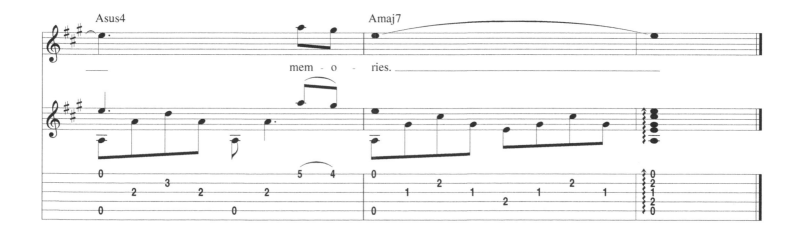

My Way

English Words by Paul Anka
Original French Words by Giles Thibault
Music by Jacques Revaux and Claude Francois

full,   I trav-eled each   and ev - 'ry high - way.   And more   much more than
course,   each care-ful step   a - long the by - way.   And more   much more than

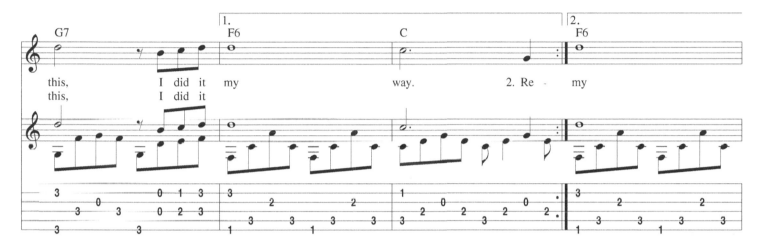

this,   I did it my   way.   2. Re -   my
this,   I did it

Bridge

way.   Yes there were times,   I'm sure you know,   when I   bit
For what is a man,   what has he   got,   if   not him -

off   more than I could chew.   But thru it   all,   when there was
self   than he has   not   to   say the   things   he tru - ly

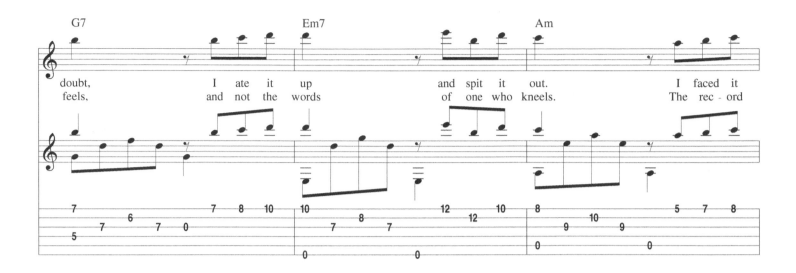

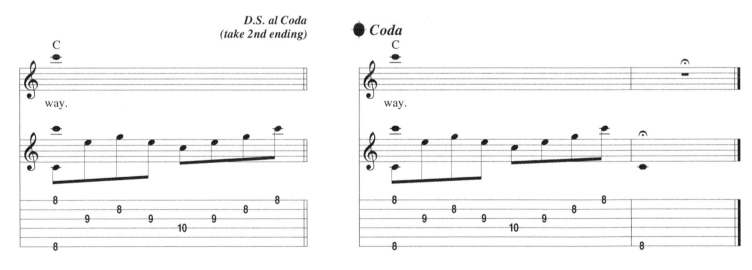

Additional Lyrics

3. I've loved, I've laughed and cried,
   I've had my fill, my share of losing.
   And now, as tears subside, I find it all so amusing.
   To think I did all that, and may I say,
   "Not in a shy way." Oh, no. Oh, no not me.
   I did it my way.

One Night

Words and Music by Dave Bartholomew and Pearl King

One night with you   is what I'm

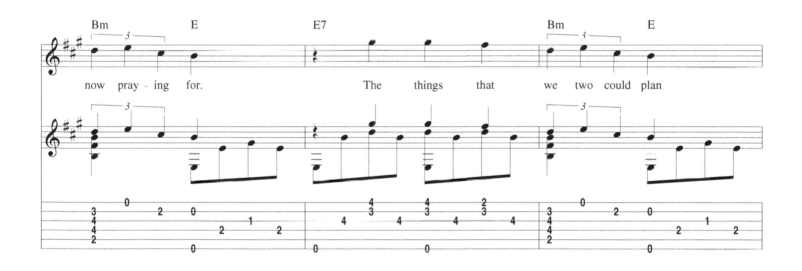

now pray-ing for.   The things that we two could plan would make my dreams come true.   Just call my

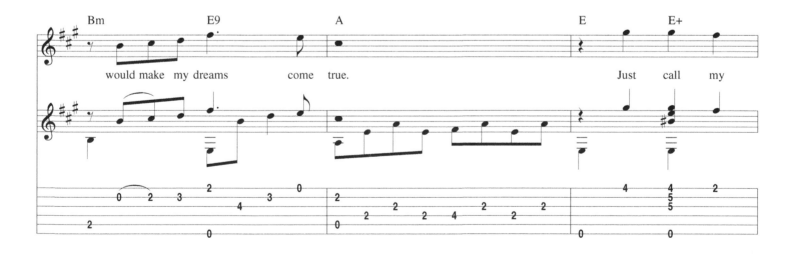

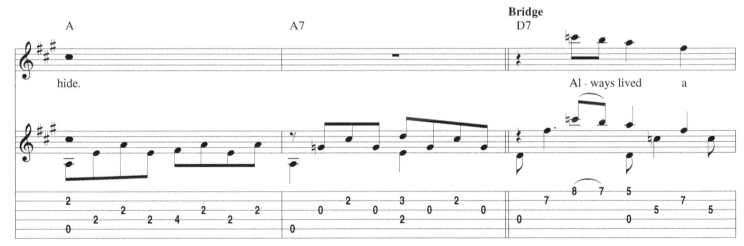

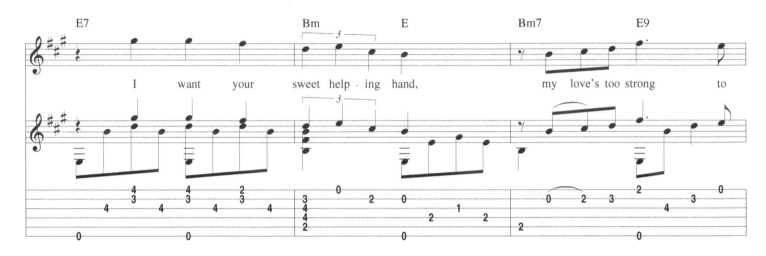

Now I know that life with-out you ___ has been ___ too ___ lone-ly too long. ___

Outro

___ One night with you ___ is what I'm

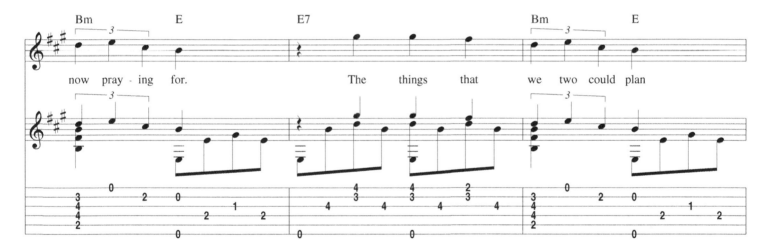

now pray-ing for. The things that we two could plan

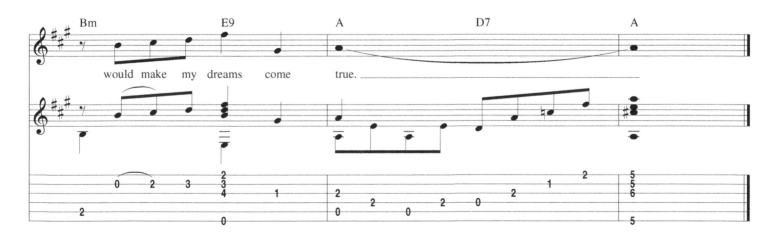

would make my dreams come true. ___

Return to Sender

Words and Music by Otis Blackwell and Winfield Scott

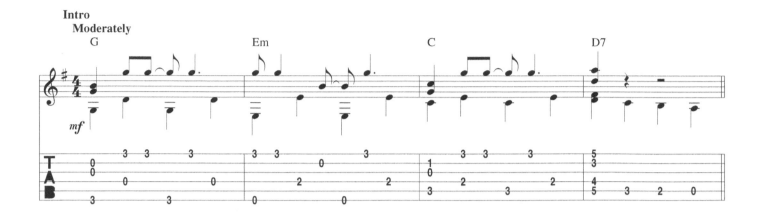

1. I gave a let-ter to the post - man; he put it in his sack.
2. So then I dropped it in the mail - box and sent it spe-cial D.

Bright and ear - ly next morn - ing he brought my let - ter back. She wrote up-on it
Bright and ear - ly next morn - ing it came right back to me.

re - turn __ to sen - der, ad - dress un - known.

To Coda

No such num - ber, no such zonc.

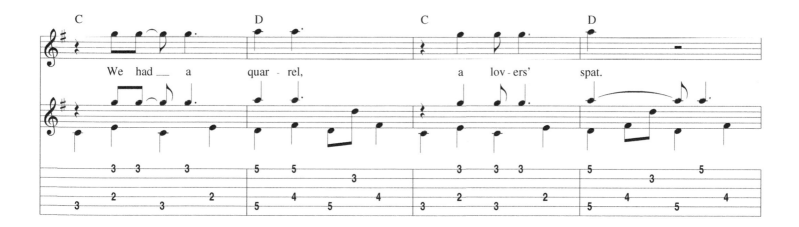

We had __ a quar - rel, a lov - ers' spat.

D.S. al Coda

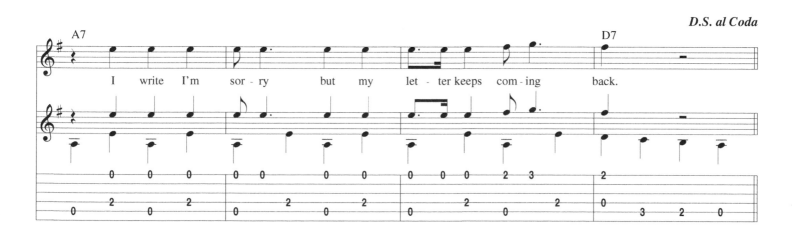

I write I'm sor - ry but my let - ter keeps com - ing back.

Bridge

This time I'm gon - na take it my - self and put it right in her hand. _____ And

if it comes back the ver - y next day, then I'll un - der - stand the writ - ing on it.

Outro

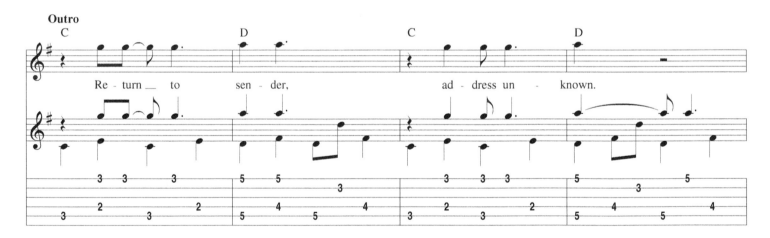

Re - turn ___ to sen - der, ad - dress un - known.

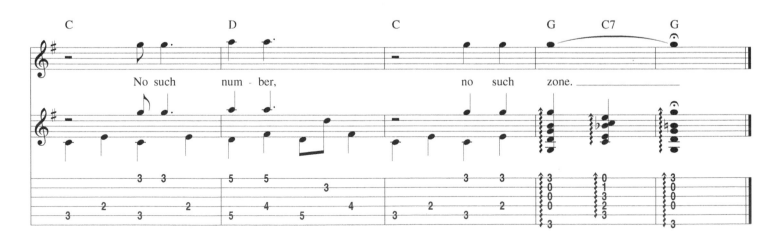

No such num - ber, no such zone. _____

Stuck on You

Words and Music by Aaron Schroeder and J. Leslie McFarland

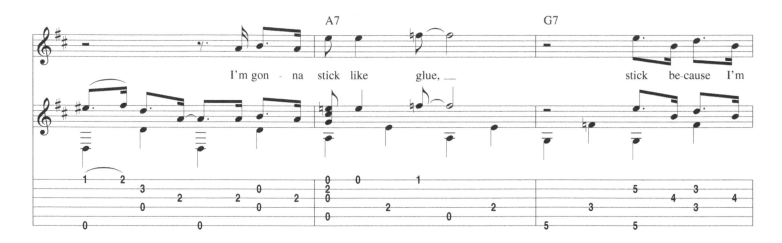

I'm gon - na stick like glue, ___ stick be-cause I'm

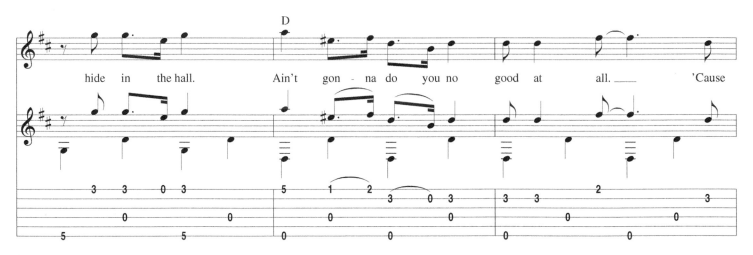

1.
stuck on you. ___

2.

Bridge

Hide in the kitch - en, ___

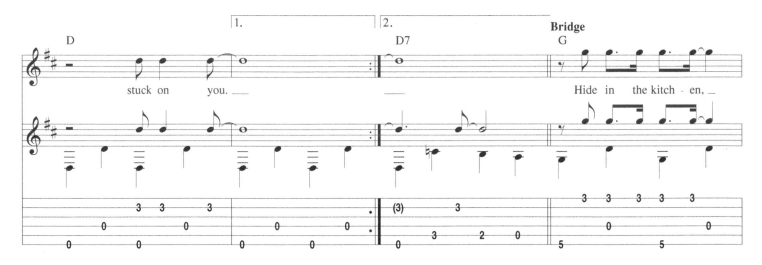

hide in the hall. Ain't gon - na do you no good at all. ___ 'Cause

once I catch ya and the kiss - in' starts, ___ a team of wild hors - es could - n't

Outro

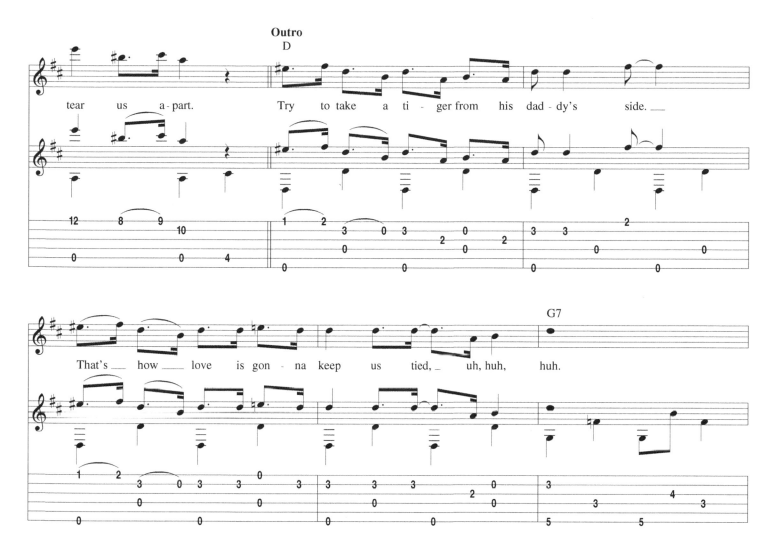

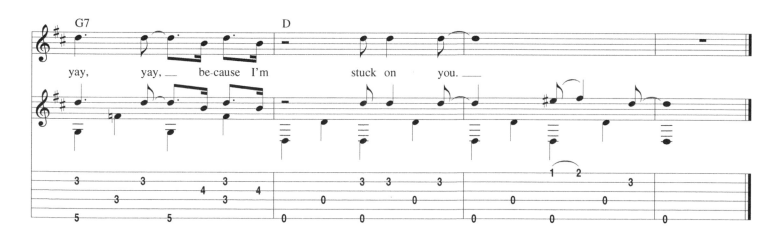

(Let Me Be Your) Teddy Bear

from LOVING YOU

Words and Music by Kal Mann and Bernie Lowe

Verse
Brightly

1. Ba - by, let me be _____ your lov - in' ted - dy bear.
2. Ba - by, let me be _____ a - round you ev - 'ry

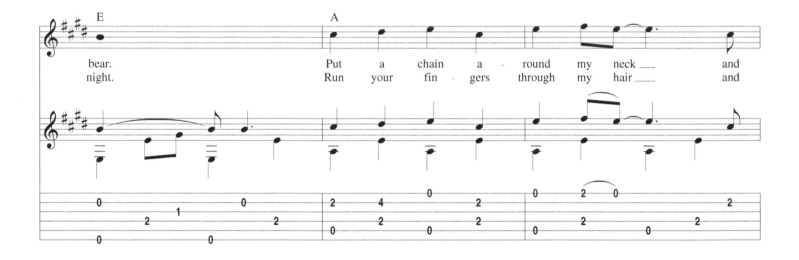

bear.   Put a chain a - round my neck _____ and
night.   Run your fin - gers round through my hair _____ and

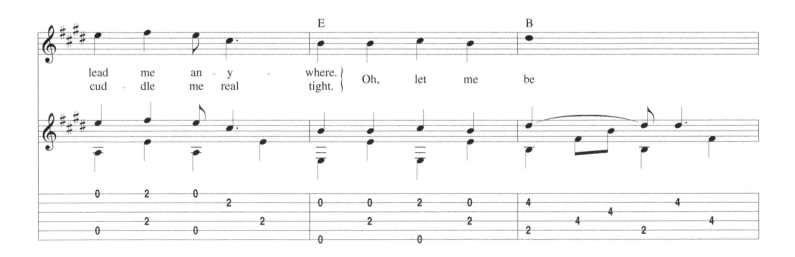

lead me an - y - where. } Oh, let me be
cud - dle me real tight.

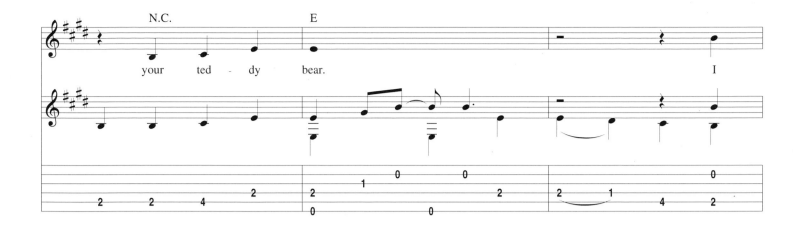

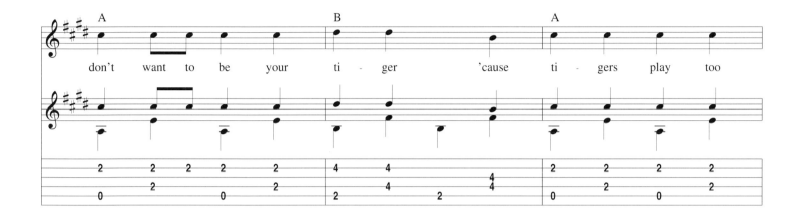

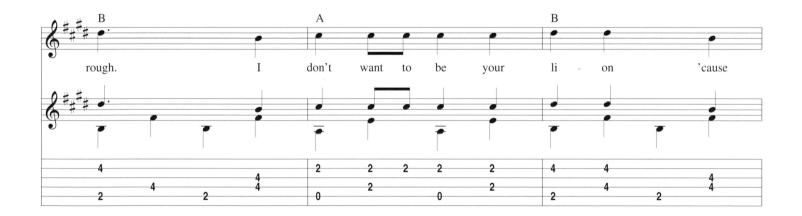

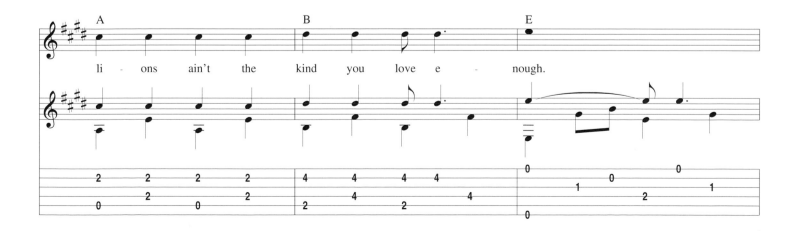

Just wan - na be your ted - dy bear. _____

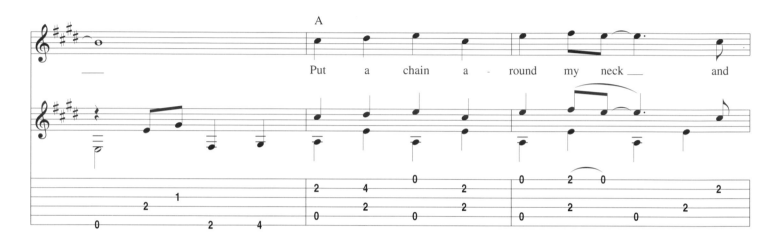

_____ Put a chain a - round my neck _____ and

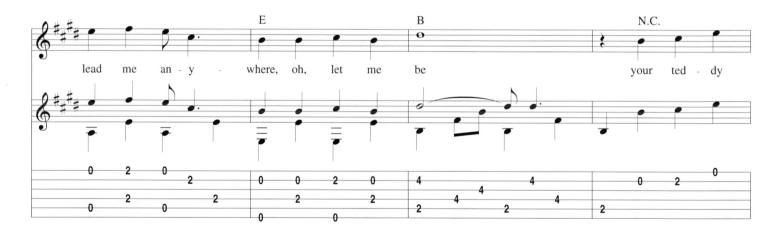

lead me an - y - where, oh, let me be your ted - dy

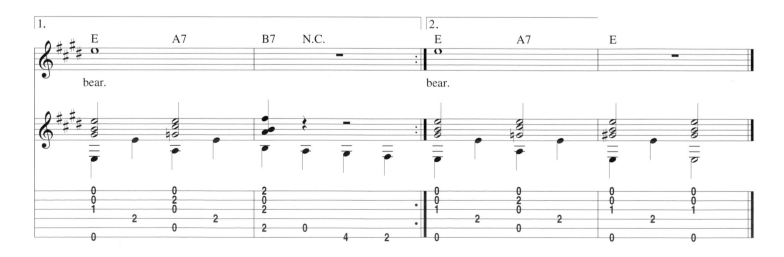

bear. bear.